# Historicity of Rāma and Kṛṣṇa

Literary, Historical, Archaeological and Scientific Perspectives

# Historicity of Rāma and Kṛṣṇa

Literary, Historical, Archaeological and Scientific Perspectives

# Historicity of Rāma and Kṛṣṇa

*Literary, Historical, Archaeological and Scientific Perspectives*

G.P. Singh

D.K. Printworld (P) Ltd.
New Delhi

**Cataloging in Publication Data — DK**
[Courtesy: D.K. Agencies (P) Ltd. <docinfo@dkagencies.com>]

**Singh, G. P. (Girish Prasad),** 1942-
Historicity of Rāma and Kṛṣṇa : literary, historical, archaeological and scientific perspectives / G.P. Singh.
p. cm.
Includes bibliographical references (p. )
Includes index.
ISBN 13: 9788124604564
ISBN 10: 8124604568

1. Rāma (Hindu deity) in literature. 2. Krishna (Hindu deity) in literature. 3. Vedic literature — History and criticism. 4. Hindu antiquities — India. 5. Hinduism and science — India. 6. India — History — To 324 BC. I. Title.

DDC 934 22

ISBN 13: 978-81-246-0456-4
ISBN 10: 81-246-0456-8
*First published in India in 2008*


*Published and printed by:*
D.K. Printworld (P) Ltd.
*Regd. Office:* 'Sri Kunj', F-52, Bali Nagar
Ramesh Nagar Metro Station
New Delhi-110 015
*Phones:* (011) 2545 3975; 2546 6019; *Fax:* (011) 2546 5926
*E-mail:* dkprintworld@vsnl.net
*Website:* www.dkprintworld.com

# Preface

THIS work aims at proving the historicity of Rāma and Kr̥ṣṇa on the basis of the literary, historical, archaeological and scientific evidence. It also proposes to dispel the hitherto existing impression of some historians and politicians that they were mythical and not historical personages.

The data available to us relating to the subject has been critically and objectively examined to discover the truth.

In historical reconstruction of the past, the antiquity of a place or person also matters. But we do not have any concrete evidence to determine the antiquity of Rāma and Kr̥ṣṇa, the places they originally belonged to, and the texts, particularly the *Rāmāyaṇa* (of Vālmīki) and the *Mahābhārata,* they are respectively described in, with absolute certainty. The dates suggested by the historians and archaeologists about them are not conclusive. Their antiquity is more higher than what is generally believed. As a matter of fact, they cannot be placed within any chronological framework. Whatever may be their antiquity, the historicity of Rāma and Kr̥ṣṇa remains.

I am thankful to Shri Susheel K. Mittal, D.K. Printworld (P) Ltd, New Delhi, for his consent to publish it.

This monograph, I believe, will be useful to historians, archaeologists, politicians, and all others, interested in the study of the subject.

# Contents

# 1

## Introduction

THE historicity of Rāma and Kṛṣṇa has long been a controversial subject. The controversy over the subject has been sparked off by the contradictory statements of some historians and politicians.

A fresh disquisition has been made into this subject on the basis of the evidence available in the early Vedic text, the *Vālmīki-Rāmāyaṇa,* the *Mahābhārata,* Purāṇas, some of the Buddhist and Jain works and other literary sources. All possible attempts have been made to examine the historical authenticity of the information culled from them. The evidence recorded in some of the Greek and Chinese sources relating to the subject are also of some use for our purpose. Some of the archaeological evidence directly related to the subject are of exceptional value. We have also placed our reliance on some of the available scientific data. Besides, there are some other reliable sources bearing on the subject. The data collected from the relevant sources have been harmonized together and interpreted scientifically so as to present a real picture of the subject. On the weight of the evidence one can prove the historicity of Rāma and Kṛṣṇa without an iota of doubt.

The statements of some historians and politicians that there was no epic age as such; the epics have no historical value and they are not for any historical purpose; Rāma and Kṛṣṇa have no place in the ancient history of India, they are imaginary characters and that there is no historical proof of their existence, can be dismissed as fanciful notions. The statements that Ayodhyā was not the birth place of Rāma and it shot into prominence not in his age but in the age of the Buddha, are also not worthy of credence. On the basis of the evidence recorded in the *Rāmāyaṇa* of Vālmīki and Purāṇas it can irrefutably be proved that Ayodhyā was the earliest capital of Kosala kingdom and Rāma was one of its rulers.

In a deliberate attempt to deny the existence of Rāma this argument is often put forward by some historians of ancient India that no signs of habitation of his period were found in the course of archaeological excavations carried out by B.B. Lal (former Director-General, Archaeological Survey of India, Delhi) at 14 different places in Ayodhyā and archaeological exploration of 17 sites and excavations of two sites there by R.C. Singh (former Director of Deptt. of Archaeology, Uttar Pradesh). In defence of such an argument it is also said that there is no carbon date for the earliest period of settlement in Ayodhyā. This fact should not be lost sight of that archaeology is not the only source of our knowledge of history and culture of India. It may also be noted here that despite the archaeological discovery of Kṛṣṇa's Dvārakā, his historicity is doubted and the validity of the archaeological findings of the discoverer, S.R. Rao, is questioned by a section of historians.

The genealogy of Ikṣvāku dynasty given in the *Rāmāyaṇa* of Vālmīki and Purāṇas has great historical value. The genealogy contains the names of kings of both pre- and post-Rāma periods who ruled the Kosala kingdom with its capital at Ayodhyā. The historicity of a number of kings who belonged to the said dynasty is proven. The historical details provided in the *Rāmāyaṇa* and Purāṇas about them have also been archaeologically confirmed. It is only the historicity of Rāma which is debated.

There is no substance in the statements of some scholars that Kr̥ṣṇa did not play any historical role. History records that Mathurā, the earliest capital of Śūrasena kingdom, was the seat of the republican government of the Yādavas headed by Kr̥ṣṇa himself. The shifting of the capital from Mathurā to Dvārakā, the next seat of government in Kr̥ṣṇa's time, is also a historical fact. These are some of the facts which can fairly be attested to by the evidence recorded in the *Mahābhārata,* Purāṇas and other reliable sources.

Rāma and Kr̥ṣṇa do find mention in some of the standard historical works. Some of the historians of ancient India have accorded them the place they deserve.

Nothing would be more absurd than to say that Rāma and Kr̥ṣṇa were mythical and not historical personages. We have literary, historical, archaeological and scientific evidence to prove their historicity.

This subject is to be treated without any bias, pride or prejudice and not to be brought within the domain of politics of history.

# 2

# Historicity of Rāma

KINGS and kingdoms they ruled are two important historical subjects. The history of both is intertwined from the point of view of their existence. The ascertainment of historical identity of a king presupposes the determination of antiquity of the kingdom with its capital ruled by him.

Ancient Ayodhyā was the earliest capital of Kosala kingdom. (*Vālmīki-Rāmāyaṇa*, Bālakāṇḍa, 5, 1-3, 5-7; *Padma Purāṇa*, Pātālakhaṇḍa, 28, 49, Uttarakhaṇḍa, 242, 41-42; *Bhāgavata Purāṇa*, IX, 8, 17-19; *Viṣṇudharmottara Purāṇa*, I, 13, 7-12; I, 240, 2; also *Brahmāṇḍa Purāṇa*, IV, 40, 91; R.P. Sharma, *Paurāṇic Kośa*, p. 29). The historical existence of Rāma and some other rulers (anterior and posterior to him) of the Sūryavaṁśa (Solar dynasty), who ruled the kingdom with its capital at Ayodhyā can be proved beyond doubt on the basis of the available evidences.

The geographical identity and hoary antiquity of Ayodhyā cannot be doubted. According to the *Vālmīki-Rāmāyaṇa*, the city of Ayodhyā was founded by the primaeval king Vaivasvata Manu. The city was 12 *yojanas* (12 × 4 = 48 *kosa* = 96 miles) in length and 3 *yojanas* (3 × 4 = 12 *kosa* = 24 miles) in breadth (Bālakaṇḍa, 5,6-8). It is described in some of the Purāṇas (*Vāyu*, I, 8, 100-07; *Viṣṇudharmottara*, I, 13, I, 12) as a great city with an extent of 10 *yojanas* and a circumference of 3 *yojanas*. According to the Jain Purāṇas (*Ādi Purāṇa* of Jinasena

III, 7, 41; *Uttara Purāṇa* of Gaṇabhadra, 71, 416; *Padma Purāṇa* of Ravisena, 3, 169-72; 81, 120; and *Harivaṁśa Purāṇa* of Jinasena II, 10, 163), it was 12 *yojanas* in length, 9 yojanas in breadth and 38 *yojanas* in circumference. In fact, the areas covered by modern Ayodhyā (on the Sarayū) and Faizabad (at a distance of about 8 km from the former), Sāketa and adjoining regions were parts of ancient Ayodhyā.

Manu's son, Ikṣvāku (a famous ancestor of Rāma) of the Solar dynasty was the first ruler of Ayodhyā which can be confirmed by the evidence adduced in the *Vālmīki-Rāmāyaṇa* (Bālakāṇḍa, 70, 21-22, also Ayodhyākāṇḍa, 49, 13); the *Mahābhārata* (Sabhā Parva, 13, 3-6); and the Purāṇas (*Brahmāṇḍa*, 3, 60, 20; *Matsya*, 12,19; *Brahma*, 7, 20; and *Paurāṇic Kośa*, pp. 52-23). In the *Rāmāyaṇa* of Vālmīki as well as in the Purāṇas the royal family of Ayodhyā is well represented as being descended from a king named Ikṣvāku. The earliest allusion to him occurs in the *Ṛgveda* (X, 60, 4). Pāṇini (fifth century BCE) in his *Aṣṭādhyāyī-Sūtra* (VI, 1, 171; VI, 4, 174); also V.S. Agrawala, *India as Known to Pāṇini*, p. 61); Patañjali (second century BCE) in his *Mahābhāṣya* (IV, 2, 104); also B.N. Puri, *India in the Time of Patañjali*, p. 74); and Kālidāsa (first century BCE) in his *Raghuvaṁśa* (VI, 71; XIII, 61,70; XIV, 55; XV, 44) also refer to king Ikṣvāku of Kosala. Kālidāsa in particular in his said work mentions some kings and princes of Ayodhyā including Aja, Dilīpa, Raghu, Sagara, Daśaratha, Rāma and his two sons Kuśa and Lava who were all descendants of Ikṣvāku.

In one of the Jaina non-canonical texts (*Vividhatīrthakalpa* of Jinaprabhasūri) it is clearly stated that Ayodhyā was also known as Ikṣvākubhūmi (the land of Ikṣvāku), Rāmapurī (the city of Rāma) and Sāketa.

There are some positive evidences to prove the historicity of Rāma. The earliest reference to him as a king occurs in the *Ṛgveda* (X, 93, 14). In the same Vedic text (I, 126, 4) his father Daśaratha also finds mention. The Ṛgvedic reference to Rāma is obviously a later addition.

The dynastic genealogies of the kings of Ikṣvāku dynasty who ruled the kingdom of Kosala with its capital at Ayodhyā provided in the *Rāmāyaṇa* and the Purāṇas constitute a substantial evidence to prove that Rāma was a historical figure. The historical credibility of the epic and Purāṇic genealogies of Ikṣvāku family to which Rāma belonged can hardly be doubted.

The genealogy provided in the *Rāmāyaṇa* of Vālmīki contains a list of 35 kings (of Ikṣvāku lineage) of Ayodhyā down to Rāma (Bālakāṇḍa, 70, 20-45; Ayodhyākāṇḍa, 110, 5-36). It is no doubt a truncated genealogy. But it does prove the historicity of Rāma. According to the Purāṇas (*Vāyu,* 88, 3-183; *Matsya,* 12, 25-37; *Viṣṇu* IV, 2, 63-66; IV, 3, 40-49; *Brahmāṇḍa,* 3, 63, 115-80; *Brahma,* 8, 28-41; also F.E. Pargiter, *Ancient Indian Historical Tradition,* pp. 90-94; G.P. Singh, *Early Indian Historical Tradition and Archaeology,* pp. 38-42; S.N. Pradhan, *Chronology of Ancient India,* pp. 118, 145), in pre-Rāma period, in the line of Ikṣvāku there were 64 kings. In the genealogical order of the descendants of Ikṣvāku shown in the Purāṇa records, Rāma distinctly figures as the sixth-fifth king of Ayodhyā. The Purāṇic genealogy in comparison to that in the *Rānāyaṇa* is, of course, more perfect and authentic. However, the reliability of the *Rāmāyaṇa* genealogy cannot be doubted. The traditional genealogies preserved in the *Rānāyaṇa* and the Purāṇas including those of ruling Ikṣvāku family of Ayodhyā are no doubt very faithful. It is said that ". . . traditional genealogies are rarely faithful records of times past." (Romila Thapar, "Genealogy as a Source of Social History," in her *Ancient Indian Social History*, p. 326.)

Of the 64 kings of Ikṣvāku dynasty who ruled the kingdom of Kosala with its capital at Ayodhyā in pre-Rāma period, Māndhātā, the son of Yuvanasva II, and his three sons, Purukutsa, Ambarīṣa and Mucukunda), Bāhu, Sagara, Dilīpa and Daśaratha were the most important. Their existence are historically proven. The details of all historical events of their times are provided in the Purāṇas and other reliable sources. (For details see Pargiter, op. cit., chap. XXIV, *Ancient History from Tradition*, pp. 261-63; G.P. Singh, op. cit., pp. 38-41).

Daśaratha, the father of Rāma was one of the powerful sovereigns of Ayodhyā. During his time, Ayodhyā had all the paraphernalia of sovereignty and pride and pomp of royalty. The Kosala kingdom during his time had friendly relations with the eastern kingdoms of Videha, Aṅga and Magadha, the Punjab kingdoms of Kekeya, Sindu and Sauvīra, the western kingdom of Saurāṣṭra, and the kingdom of Kāśī in the middle region of north India. Daśaratha was succeeded by Rāma who was the real and the last famous sovereign of Ayodhyā. In his time, Ayodhyā was popularly known as Rāmanagar (city of Rāma) as it is stated in one of the Purāṇas (*Brahmāṇḍa*, 3, 37, 33; 3, 47, 75; 3, 48, 1). His period constituted a watershed in the politico-cultural history of Ayodhyā. His reign witnessed all-round progress and prosperity of Ayodhyā, the capital city of Kosala kingdom. His benevolent rule is fully described in the Ayodhyākāṇḍa of *Vālmīki-Rāmāyaṇa*.

During his rule, he took several measures to promote the welfare of the people of his state. The modern concept of welfare state is believed to have sprung forth from the ancient ideals of Rāmarājya. He was married to Sītā, the daughter of king Janaka of Videha. That matrimonial relation brought the two kingdoms — Kosala and Videha — closer to each other. Some sort of political and diplomatic relations were maintained between the two kingdoms. The capital of Videha kingdom was Mithilā also called Janakapura, now lying within the border of Nepal.

On the testimony of *Skanda Purāṇa* (Vaiṣṇava Khaṇḍa, Ayodhyā Mahātmya, chs. I and 10) it can be proved without an iota of doubt that Ayodhyā was the birth-place of Rāma, one of the lineal descendants of Ikṣvāku of Sūryavaṁśa. The Purāṇic evidence can also be corroborated by the statement of N.S. Rajaram, a scientist and historian. ("Distortions of Indian History from Haṛappā to Ayodhyā," *The Astrological Magazine,* Bangalore, vol. 87, no. I, January 1998, p. 76).

Following the hereditary line of royal succession all necessary arrangements were made for the accession of Rāma (being the eldest son of Daśaratha) to the throne of Ayodhyā. It was public will to install Rāma as the king that prompted king Daśaratha to make him his successor. He consulted the council of ministers including the chief priest about the proposed consecration of Rāma. But in the meantime some other developments took place. In order to keep his word he gave to Kaikeyī (one of his three wives) just to please her, he had to nominate her son Bharata his heir-apparent and exile Rāma for fourteen years. During the exile period of Rāma Rāmacandra), his sandals (wooden one) ruled and Bharata acted only as its regent considering the former (his elder brother) a legitimate or rightful successor to the throne. This was very much in conformity with one of the ethics of ancient Indian polity that the throne is never to be kept vacant due to the fear of anarchy of a kingless state (*arājaka rājya*). The details concerning the above have been provided not only in the

*Rāmāyaṇa* of Vālmīki (Ayodhyākāṇḍa, I, 1-51; Cantos 2-18, 39 67, 112-114) but also in one of the Purāṇas (*Agni* 6, 2-6, 24 and 51). The popular tradition and belief also affirm what is recorded in the said epic and Purāṇa.

The places (including Śṛṅgaverapura, Bhāradvāja Āśrama and Citrakūṭa) visited by Rāma in the course of his wanderings during the exile period have also been traced by an eminent historian and archaeologist, Maheshwari Prasad (Prof., Deptt. of Ancient Indian History, Culture and Archaeology). His archaeological findings are quite consistent with Vālmīki's description of Rāma's sojourns at various places in the course of his wanderings.

The coronation ceremony of Rāma as a king took place on his return to Ayodhyā after the conquest of Laṅkā and his victory over Rāvaṇa. (*Vālmīki-Rāmāyaṇa,* Yuddhakāṇḍa, also called Laṅkākāṇḍa, 131, 1-115.) As noted before, he was the 65th king of Ayodhyā. This event is stated to be a part of *purātana itihāsa* (ancient history) in the text itself. (Ibid., 131, 116.)

In his *Rāmāyaṇa,* Vāmīlki has furnished the details of how Rāma got the stone bridge built on the sea (commonly known as Rāma-Setu) for taking his army to Laṅkā to attack it and fight its king Rāvaṇa. (Yuddhakāṇḍa, also called Laṅkākāṇḍa 22, 47-89 23, 1-16; see also cantos 1-115.) That bridge is now under sea situated south-east of Rāmeśwaram. It is not mythical but a man-made structure.

The literary description of Rāma-Setu can be confirmed by scientific evidence. Some attempts have, of course, been made by space scientists from NASA to prove the existence of Rāma. "The clinching evidence about the reality of Śrī Rāma's existence was provided by the Indian Satellite IRS-IA in 1962 which gave to the world the first photograph taken from space showing the remnants of the Stone Bridge (*setu*) that Rāma had built on the sea to take his army to Rāvaṇa's Laṅkā. It had appeared as a streak connecting Dhanuṣkoṭi (or Arichalmunai) with Talaimannar coast (of Laṅkā). However, when on 14.9.1966 the Gemini-XI Satellite went into space, the US Astronauts brought back vastly clear and vivid photographs of remnants of that *setu*." (*The Challenge of Truth*, Delhi, 2001, p. 4.) Those photographs have been published by the National Geographical Society (see Ibid., the back cover page).

The identification and location of Laṅkā described in the *Vālmīki-Rāmāyaṇa* has been the subject of debate among the scholars. However, the two Ceylonese Pāli chronicles — *Dīpavaṁśa* (fourth century CE) and *Mahāvaṁśa* (fifth century CE) — attest to the fact that Laṅkā was the local name of the island of Ceylon. H.D. Sankalia, an archaeologist of international repute, has also identified Laṅkā in the *Rāmāyaṇa* with ancient Ceylon or Laṅkā changed to Sri Lanka. ("Antiquity of the Name Sri Lanka," in his *Aspects of Indian History and Archaeology*, pp. 209-10.)

We have a numismatic evidence to testify to the existence of Rāma. A copper utensil full of silver coins which was dscovered from the river-bed at Khanaut in Uttar Pradesh some time back contained 20 coins bearing the name of Rāma and depiction of Sūrya (sun) which stands for Solar family which he belonged to. Some of these coins were issued by Rāma's brother Bharata during the exile period of the former. This is proved by the fact that some of the coins have on the reverse side the emblem of double sandal (originally made of wood) of Rāma which king (*de facto*) Bharata worshipped during his brother's exile period for the reason known to all of us. The discovery of the said coins was brought to light by Dr Fateh Singh, former Director of Rajasthan Prachya Vidya Pratishthan, Jodhpur. (For facsimile of such coins see *Organiser*, 6 January, 1991.)

There is also an epigraphic evidence to prove the historicity of Rāma. In the Nasik Inscription of a Sātavāhana king Vāśiṣṭhiputra Pulumāvi (CE 131-59), Rāma finds mention along with other kings — Nābhāga, Nahuṣa, Yayāti and Sagara.

We do not have archaeological evidence (epigraphic or numismatic) of more reliable character regarding the historicity of Rāma. However, we have some other archaeological evidences in this regard as shown here later in appropriate places.

In pre-Bhārata war period, all the descendants of Ikṣvāku down to Rāma ruled Kosala kingdom with its capital at Ayodhyā.

H.D. Sankalia was of the view that the antiquity of the places occurring in the *Mahābhārata* and Purāṇas can be proved with the help of archaeology. He felt that "A similar attempt should now be made to test the principal places associated with Rāma such as Ayodhyā. If the story is correct, many of the places which Rāma visited during his fourteen years' exile were in forests or such sparsely inhabited localities. So our efforts to be successful should be directed to Rāma's capital, and its vicinity, the Sarayū Valley, or the ancient Kosala. The region to the south called south (Dakṣiṇa) Kosala might yield equally old but different cultural relics." ("Archaeology and Tradition", in his *Aspects of Indian History and Archaeology*, p. 278.) Attempts have, of course, been made by some archaeologists in this direction, but it has not yet been possible for them to find out the habitation layer of the period to which Rāma belonged. Until and unless that layer is found in the course of archaeological excavations at Ayodhyā and the carbon-14 dates on the basis of the testing of some samples of that period are obtained, no definite date of its antiquity or of the period of Rāma can be suggested. We have no carbon dates of the earliest period of settlements at Ayodhyā. In fact, it has been found difficult to determine the exact antiquity of the places and persons described in the *Rāmāyaṇa* of Vālmīki, *Mahābhārata* and Purāṇas. Generally, they are found to have existed much earlier to the dates suggested by archaeologists. The dates suggested by historians and archaeologists are generally found at variance with each other.

The hypothesis of Rāma living in Ayodhyā some time early in the first millennium BCE cannot be accepted. According to Sankalia, his period falls in between *c.* 2350-1950 BCE. ("Prehistoric Colonization in India: Archaeological and Literary Evidence," in *Aspects of Indian History and Archaeology*, p. 304.)

Sankalia had anticipated as far back as 1975 that "Ayodhyā when excavated should give us thick deposits and the earliest should go back to at least 2500 BCE." (*Aspects of Indian History and Archaeology*, p. 304.) But this has not yet come true.

There have been no systematic and extensive archaeological excavations in and around Ayodhyā till today. However, some scrappy excavations were carried out at Ayodhyā in the late 1960s and 1970s. Archaeological explorations have also been undertaken here from time to time. Between 1975 and 1980 as many as 14 different places in Ayodhyā including those three in the vicinity of the so-called Rāmajanmabhūmi (birth-place of Rāma) were excavated under the direction of an internationally renowned archaeologist B.B. Lal (former Director-General, Archaeological Survey of India) which were a part of his large project called "Archaeology of the Rāmāyaṇa sites." His discoveries as well as those of other archaeologists throw light on the history of Ayodhyā of post-Rāma period which do not fall within the scope of this work.

Rāma's Ayodhyā depicted in the *Rāmāyaṇa* in a true historical perspective was a city of primaeval antiquity. V.A. Smith has correctly stated that ". . . the ancient city of Ayodhyā famous as the capital of Rāma was replaced by the modern city of Faizabad. The latter was built in no small degree from the materials of Rāma's capital." (*Catalogue of the Coins in the Indian Museum*, Calcutta, vol. 1, *Coins of Ancient India*, p. 144, see also pp. 148-51.) A. Cunningham's description in this regard is very graphic and elaborate. He visited Ayodhyā and the neighbouring town of Faizabad (about 8 km away from the former) some time between 1862 and 1865 to find an archaeological evidence about Ayodhyā of Rāma's time. He observes: "The present city of Ayodhyā, which is confined to the north-east corner of the old site is just two miles in length by about three quarters of a mile in breadth, but not one half of this extent is occupied by buildings, and the whole place wears a look of decay. There are no high mounds of ruins, covered with broken statues and sculptured pillars, such as mark the sites of other ancient cities, but only a low irregular mass of rubbish heaps from which all the bricks have been excavated for the houses of the neighbouring city of Faizabad. This Muhammedan city, which is 2½ miles in length by 1 mile in breadth, is built chiefly of materials extracted from the ruins of Ayodhyā. The two cities together occupy an area of nearly 6 sq. miles, or just about one half of the probable size of the ancient capital of Rāma." (*The Ancient Geography of India*, p. 342; *Archaeological Survey of India, Reports*, vol. 1. Shimla, 1871, p. 321.)

In an attempt to deny the existence of Rāma, some historians writing, of ancient India, came out with the statements in the recent past that the birth place of Rāma in Ayodhyā was not identifiable; Rāma was a mythical figure; and that Ayodhyā rose into prominence in the age of the Buddha (sixth and fifth centuries BCE) and not in the age of Rāma.

The birth-place of Rāma has already been identified. Rāma was not a mythical but a historical figure. Ayodhyā had already come into prominence in the age of Rāma. In pre-Bhārata war period, from Ikṣvāku down to Rāma, Ayodhyā constantly remained the capital of the Kosala kingdom. In the epic and Purāṇic tradition, Ayodhyā seems to have been the earliest capital of the said kingdom, and in the Buddhist tradition Sāketa the next. From one of the Pāli cononical texts (*Dīgha-Nikāya*, II, p. 146) it is quite evident that in the time of the Buddha, Sāketa and Śrāvastī were the important cities and not Ayodhyā. It has been rightly said that "In Buddha's time Ayodhyā sank to the level of an unimportant city but Sāketa and Śrāvastī were two of the six important cities of India." (B.C. Law, "Countries and Peoples of India, Epic and Paurāṇic Sources" in his *Geographical Essays Relating to Ancient Geography of India*, p. 130; *Geography of Early Buddhism*, p. 5; *Annals of the Bhandarkar Oriental Research Institute*, Poona, vol. XVII, pt. III, 1935-36, pp. 225*ff*; "The Kosalas in Ancient India," *Indian Historical Quarterly*, vol. 1, nos. 1-2, Delhi, 1979, pp. 139-65; see also his article on Ayodhyā in *Journal of Ganganath Jha Research Institute*, Allahabad, vol. 1, pp. 423-43).

Ayodhyā and Sāketa like Kāśī-Vārāṇaṣī were the twin cities. That is why both have been identified with each other. Kālidāsa regards both Ayodhyā (*Raghuvaṁśa*, XI, 93; XIII,61; XIV, 29; XV, 38, 60 98; XVI, 25; XVII, 36) and Sāketa (Ibid., V, 31; XIII, 79; XIV, 13; XVIII; 36) as the same capital city of the Ikṣvāku kngs of Kosala. In the Jaina canonical tradition, in place of Ayodhyā, Sāketa has been mentioned as the capital of the Kosala kingdom. (J.C. Jain, *Life in Ancient India as depicted in Jaina Canon and Commentaries,* p. 337). In his *Abhidhānacintāmaṇi* (p. 222), Hemacandra (a Jain Scholar of the twelfth century) refers to Ayodhyā and Sāketa as the same city.

It is significant to note that in the post-Bhārata war period, the Ikṣvāku dynasty ruled the kingdom of Kosala with its capital at Śrāvastī alone till the fifth century BCE. In Buddha's time, Śrāvastī became famous as the capital city of Kosala kingdom. (See also B.B. Lal, "Ayodhyā of the *Vālmīki-Rāmāyaṇa:* An Enjoying Debate on its Identification," *Purātattva,* Journal of the Indian Archaeological Society, No. 16, 1985-86, pp. 79-84.)

The historical details available about Bharata, Lakṣmaṇa and Śatrughna in the *Rāmāyaṇa,* Purāṇas and other reliable sources also show that their eldest brother Rāma did exist. Bharata obtained the Kekaya kingdom (the province of his mother Kaikeyī) in the western Punjab between Gandhāra and the Beās, and also Upper Sindh. The capital of the Kekayas has been identified with Girjak or Jalalpur on the river Jhelum. Bharata also conquered Gandhāra and founded Takṣaśilā and Puṣkaravatī (also called Puṣkalavatī). Lakṣmaṇa had two sons, Aṅgada and Candraketu. The former was the ruler of Malla-deśa and the latter of Candrāvatī. Śatrughna ruled Śūrasena Janapada with its capital at Mathurā, founded by himself. (See G.P. Singh, *Early Indian Historical Tradition and Archaeology,* pp. 42-43.)

The available literary and archaeological evidence regarding the rule of Rāma's two sons, Kuśa and Lava, over the south Kosala with its capital at Kuśāvatī and the north Kosala with its capital at Śrāvastī respectively following the territorial divisions of the kingdom of Kosala into two parts — Dakṣiṇa Kosala and Uttara Kosala — also go to prove the historicity of their father.

According to *Vālmīki-Rāmāyaṇa* (Uttarakāṇḍa, 107, 17; 108, 4; also R.K. Rai, *Vālmīki-Rāmāyaṇa Kośa,* p. 73) and the Purāṇas (*Vāyu,* 88, 198-200; *Brahmāṇḍa* 3, 63, 188-91; *Matsya,* 12, 40-44; *Viṣṇu,* IV, 4, 104; *Padma,* VI, 208, 46-47; VI, 271, 10-2; also *Paurāṇic Kośa,* pp. 121-33), Kuśa being the eldest son of Rāma succeeded him and later became ruler of south Kosala with its capital at Kuśāvatī (also called Kuśasthalī) founded by Rāma himself at the foot of the Vindhya mountain. There is a perfect harmony between the epic and Purāṇic evidence regarding this aspect of the subject. Kālidāsa also mentions Kuśa (*Raghuvaṁśa,* XV, 32, 63, 97; XVI, 14, 72, 81, 88; XVII, 4; XVIII, 4) and his capital Kuśāvatī (Ibid., XV 97; XVI, 25; also S.C. Banerji, *Kālidāsa-Kośa,* p. 28). The *Kuśa Jātaka* refers to Kuśa (in the line of Okkaku = Ikṣvāku of Pāli canon) as a king of Kuśāvatī (identical with modern Kuśīnagara in the Malla country. (G.P. Malalasekera, *Dictionary of Pāli Proper Names,* vol. 1, p. 653.)

According to Cunningham, the ancient Kuśāvatī, identical with Kuśapura (*Kia-she-pu-lo* of Hiuen Tsang) or Kuśabhavanapura, was named after Rāma's son Kuśa. He says, "The site of Kuśapura was, no doubt, selected by its founder as a good military position on account of its being surrounded on three sides by the river Gomatī." (*Ancient Geography of India,* p. 337.) He found the place utterly desolate. He identifies it with an old town of Sultanpur on the Gomatī at a distance of 28 or 30 miles from the present city of Ayodhyā in the north which is just six miles in excess of the distance given by Hiuen Tsang. He further adds that "The ruined fort of Sultanpur now forms a large mound, 750 ft square, with brick towers at the four corners. On all sides it is surrounded by the huts of the ruined town, the whole together covering a space of about half a mile square, or about two miles in circuit. This estimate of the size of Sultanpur agrees very closely with that of Kuśapura given by Hiuen Tsang, who describes the place as being 10 *li* or 1 $^{2}/_{3}$ miles, in circuit." (Ibid.) V.A. Smith has located Kuśapura in Unnao district. (Cf. Thomas Watters, *On Yuan Chwang's Travels in India,* II, p. 339.)

After the death of his father Rāma, Kuśa shifted his capital from Kuśāvatī to Ayodhyā from where South Kosala was governed by him and his successors who sixteen in number.

That Rāma installed his son Lava as the ruler of the kingdom of Uttara Kosala with its capital at Śrāvastī can be proved by the evidence furnished in the *Vālmīki-Rāmāyaṇa* (Uttarakāṇḍa, 107, 5, 17), Purāṇas (*Vāyu,* 88, 199-200; *Viṣṇu,* IV, 4, 104-05) and the *Raghuvaṁśa* of Kālidāsa (XV, 32, 63, 97; *Kālidāsa Kośa,* p 30). In the line of Lava there were fifteen kings after him down to Bṛhadbala in pre-Bhārata war period.

The epic and Purāṇic tradition regarding the two great divisions of the Kosala kingdom — north and south Kosala — can be supported by the Buddhist tradition recorded in the *Avadānaśataka.* (Cf. R.L. Mitra, *Sanskrit Buddhist Literature of Nepal,* p. 20.)

According to Purāṇic evidence, the city of Śrāvastī situated on the right bank of the Acirāvatī (modern Rāptī) was originally founded in pre-Rāma period by a king named Śrāvasta, the son of Yuvanāsva I, one of the descendants of Ikṣvāku. (*Vāyu,* 88, 24-27; *Matsya,* 12, 29-30; *Viṣṇu,* IV, 2, 36-37; see also B.C. Law, "Śrāvastī in Ancient Indian Literature," *Memoirs of the Archaeological Survey of India,* No. 50, Delhi, 1935, pp. 9f.) Supporting the Purāṇic evidence, Cunningham ascribes the foundation of the celebrated capital city Śrāvastī (northward of Sāketa or Ayodhyā) to Śrāvasta who ascended the throne of Ayodhyā anterior to Rāma. He also admits that during the early period it formed a part of the kingdom of Ayodhyā. He has identified it with the ruined city of Sahet-Mahet on the south bank of Rāptī situated between Akāonā and Balaramapur at 5 miles from the former and 12 miles from the latter and at nearly equal distance from Bahraich and Goṇḍā. The exact distance of this ruined city from Ayodhyā, according to him, is 58 miles. (*Ancient Geography of India*, pp. 343-46; *Archaeological Survey of India, Reports*, I, p. 331.) The kingdom of Kosala approximately coinciding with the Sarayū-Rāptī doab contained three principal cities — Ayodhyā, Sāketa and Śrāvastī.

Archaeologically, the existence of Śrāvastī was proved as far back as 1907-08 in the course of the excavations carried out there under the guidance of Sir John Marshal and Daya Ram Sahani. (*Archaeological Survey of India, Annual Reports*, 1907-08, p. 84.)

Śrāvastī was visited by Fa-hien in CE 400. (H.A. Giles (tr.), *A Record of the Buddhistic Kingdoms: An Account of the Travels of Fa-hien*, pp. 30-31.) Hiuen Tsang visited this capital city (called by him *Shih-lo-fa-si-ti*) in CE 632. He found it almost deserted. He says that the old foundations of the palace city were above twenty *li* in circuit. (T. Watters, op. cit., I, p. 377.)

The Purāṇa records bear eloquent testimony to the fact that Gautama Buddha (earlier called Siddhārtha), the son of Śuddhodana of the Śākya family of Kosala, was descendant of the ruler of the same Ikṣvāku dynasty to which Rāma himself belonged. In the Purāṇic genealogical list of thirty kings of the said dynasty (in the line of Rāma's son Lava, the king of Śrāvastī) who ruled Kosala with its capital at Śrāvastī from the time the Great Bhārata war came to end to the fifth century BCE, the pedigree and progeny of Buddha are given. He (Buddha) figures in the list as the twenty-fourth king. His grandfather, Śākya (the twenty-second king in the list), founded a new sub-dynasty called Śākya dynasty and became the ruler of the north-western portion of Kosala kingdom (after its disintegration) lying at the foot of the Himalaya mountain adjoining Nepal with its capital at Kapilavastu. In the same genealogical list, Prasenajit, the famous ruler of Kosala (with its capital at Śrāvastī) and a contemporary of Budddha, figures as the twenty-sixth king. (*Vāyu*, 99, 280-93; *Matsya*, 271, 4-18; 273, 52-53; *Viṣṇu*, IV, 22, 1-13; *Brahmāṇḍa*, 3, 74, 104-10; also Pargiter, *The Purāṇa Text of the Dynasties of the Kali Age*, pp. 66-67; G.P. Singh, *Early Indian Historical Tradition and Archaeology*, pp. 146-48.) The historicity of Buddha, Prasenajit and some other rulers of the said dynasty have so far not been doubted by any scholar. But why the historicity of Rāma who also belonged to the same dynasty is often doubted by some historians of ancient India and others, we fail to understand. We see no reason to doubt his historicity.

The historicity of Rāma can be proved also with the help of the evidence recorded in some Buddhist works. In his two famous works, *Buddhacarita* (a biography of the Buddha) and *Saundarānanda* (an epic), Aśvaghoṣa, a native of Sāketa (Ayodhyā) and a celebrated Buddhist scholar who adorned the court of Kaniṣka (CE 78-125), has depicted Rāma as a historical personage. In his former work (I, 1), he has mentioned him as a king of Ayodhyā. In his latter work (I, 24), he has unequivocally stated that Rāma and Buddha (the two great historical personalities) belonged to the same Ikṣvāku dynasty, which goes well in accord with Purāṇic evidence. He has also narrated the stories connected with the lives and activities of

Rāma's two sons — Kuśa and Lava — in both of his works, *Buddhacarita* (I, 43) and *Saundarānanda* (I, 26).

Rāma, no doubt, occupies an important place in the history of ancient India. What R.S. Tripathi, one of the noted authorities on ancient Indian history, has stated about him is also worthy of our attention. He says: ". . . Kosala was an important kingdom in *Madhyadeśa* ever since Āryan expansion eastwards . . . the nucleus of fact is that Rāma was a real person, who belonged to the royal Ikṣvāku house of Ayodhyā, and whose achievements both in war and peace left a deep impression upon the popular imagination. The epoch of Rāma's beneficent rule is, however, as uncertain as the contemporary political condition of northern or southern India." (*History of Ancient India,* p. 65.)

The historical existence of Rāma can irrefutably be proved on the combined testimony of literature, history, archaeology and science.

# 3

# Historicity of Kṛṣṇa

KṚṢṆA was born at Mathurā. He was the son of Vasudeva. He was a multi-faceted personality. He combined in himself the qualities of a ruler, philosopher, statesman and diplomat. He virtually flourished in the pre-Bhārata war period.

He first appeared on the political scene as the ruler of Śūrasena state with its capital at Mathurā. He was the chief of a republican state of the Andhakas and Vṛṣṇis who belonged to the Yādava clan. In his time, there were 98 leading *kula*s or families of the Andhaka-Vṛṣṇis. According to the *Mahābhārata* (Śānti Parva, 82, 8-18, 25-27, 29; Sabhā Parva 48, 42), the Andhakas and Vṛṣṇis formed a confederation (*saṁgha*) popularly known as Andhaka-Vṛṣṇi Saṁgha. They reposed their full faith in the leadership of Kṛṣṇa who belonged to the Vṛṣṇi family of Mathurā. The said *saṁgha* was more or less a type of federal republic whose antiquity can be traced back to a period preceding the outbreak of the Great Bhārata war (generally called Mahābhārata war). That was one of the oldest republics of ancient India. The Purāṇas contain numerous allusions to the Andhaka-Vṛṣṇis. (*Vāyu*, 96, 1-90; *Bhāgavata*, I, 3, 23; I, 8, 41; IX, 23, 30; IX, 24, 6-45; X, 90, 46, etc.; *Brahmāṇḍa*, 3, 71, 1-85; *Matsya*, 44, 45-85; *Viṣṇu*, IV, 13, 1-10, 19-20, 35-70; and *Brahma* 14, 14-25; 16, 9-49.) The Andhaka-Vṛṣṇi Saṁgha also finds mention in Pāṇini's *Aṣṭādhyāyī* (IV, 1, 114; VI, 2, 34). Kauṭilya (*Arthaśāstra*, I, 6, 3) mentions only Vṛṣṇi Saṁgha. It is said that the Andhaka-Vṛṣṇis "had contracted a political marriage between their families." (K.P. Jayaswal, *Hindu Polity: A Constitutional History of India in Hindu Times*, Pt II, App. A, p. 355.) In the age of the *Mahābhārata,* Mathurā on the Yamunā was under the rule of the Yādavas under the leadership of Kṛṣṇa. It was the original seat of the government.

In the Śānti Parva (82,25) of the *Mahābhārata,* Kṛṣṇa has been distinctly mentioned as *saṁghamukhya* (the Head of the Andhaka-Vṛṣṇi Saṁgha). He was elected by all the members of the Assembly as president of the *saṁgha.* Āhuka (on the side of the Vṛṣṇi) and Akrūra (on the side of the Andhakas) were the leaders of two different political parties in the *saṁgha sabhā* (Federal Assembly) or joint *saṁgha* (Federal Parliament). (Śānti Parva, 82, 10; also Jayaswal, op. cit.; p. 355.) Discussions and deliberations were held in the Assembly or Parliament under the presidentship of Kṛṣṇa in the best tradition of the republic. As the President of a republican state he says, "he is not the master but the slave (of the Central Assembly) as he has to listen patiently to the bitter criticisms of the different parties. He is entitled only to half of the executive powers." (Śānti Parva, 82, 5.) This shows that supreme authority was not vested in him. The power was jointly shared by him and the members of the House which is one of the characteristic features of a republican system of government. As the head or president of the *saṁgha* he was the highest executive officer, and all the members of the executive assisted him in the execution of policies and programmes. (Ibid., 82, 16-18; see also 82, 25-27; 108, 8, 13-14.) In the context of leadership of Kṛṣṇa, it has been remarked that in the *Mahābhārata* period a new tendency grew up among the people to place themselves under the protection of individual leaders for better defence against external aggression. (U.N. Ghoshal, *A History of Indian Political Ideas*, pp. 239-40.)

A numismatic evidence regarding Kṛṣṇa also deserves our notice. An inscribed silver coin of the Vṛṣṇis datable to the first century BCE (now in the British Museum) was discovered by Cunningham. The symbol depicted on the reverse side of the coin stands for "*Sudarśanacakra* (discus) of *rājanya* (leader) Kṛṣṇa." (*Coins of Ancient India from the Earliest Times down to the Seventh Century* CE, p. 70, pl. IV; also J. Allan, *A Catalogue of the Indian Coins in the British Museum, Ancient India,* pp. clvi-clvii, 281.)

Kṛṣṇa was elected the president of the Federal Assembly at Mathurā, the capital of a republican state of the Yādavas, in accordance with the provisions of the republican constitution of the time. The same system prevailed in the city-state of Nysa — a republican state to the west of the Indus in the Kabul valley near the Mount Meros. It was governed by a body consisting of 300 members and a president (chief) named Akouphis (according to the republican constitution of the state) at the time of Alexander's invasion of north-west India as recorded by one of his historians, Arrian, in his *Anabasis* (V, I & II).

Mathurā was under constant attacks from Jarāsandha, a king of Magadha, and the existence of the Yādavas was in jeopardy. Kṛṣṇa, therefore, decided to shift the capital to a safer place. And thus the capital was shifted from Mathurā in the north to Dvārakā in the west in the pre-Bhārata war period itself.

The evidence recorded in the *Mahābhārata* (Āraṇyaka Parva, 16, 1-4, 19) and Purāṇas [*Matsya,* 12, 21-22; 13, 38; 69, 9; *Vāyu,* 86, 24-28; 88, 199; 96, 46, 57-66, 83-93, 111-42, up to 258; *Viṣṇu,* IV, I, 62-64 & 91; V, 23, 9-15; V, 24, 5-7; V, 33, 10; V, 37, 22-39, 42-63; V, 38, 34-35; *Harivaṁśa* (Viṣṇu Parva), 34, 1-12; 35, 1-111; 36, 1-40; 39, 10-32; *Bhāgavata,* I, 10, 1-36; I, XI, 11-12; I, 14,

25; IX, 3, 1-2, 27-36; X, 50, 1-19, 23-58; X, 52, 1-17; X, 53, 5-22; X, 58, 12; X, 80, 8-12; XI, 30, 4-48; *Brahmāṇḍa*, 3, 61, 18-23; 3, 71, 48, 62, 85; *Brahma*, 7, 28-32; 14, 53-56; 195, 1-12; *Agni*, 273, 12; *Padma*, Uttarakhaṇḍa, 246, 40-45; *Brahmavaivartta* (Uttarakhaṇḍa), 103, 7-33 & 80; and *Skanda*, (Prabhāsa Khaṇḍa) (44 chs on Dvārakā), also 4, 52], shows that Kṛṣṇa along with the Yādavas, including the Andhakas and Vṛṣṇis, moved to the west and founded a new city of Dvārakā at the old site of the earliest capital of Ānarttadeśa (modern Gujarat) near Raivatagiri (i.e. Jūnāgaṛh, ancient Girinār or Girinagara) not far off the sea-coast. The city was also called Dvāravatī (as it had many gates), Ānarttapurī, Dvārakāpurī and Vṛṣṇiandhakapurī. It was the second capital of the Yādavas. It was a densely populated city.

We are further told that Dvārakā was a well-planned and fortified city. It was adorned with palatial buildings with domes and minarets, temples, gates, spacious roads, streets, market-complex, the assembly hall of the Yādavas, etc. It was guarded by soldiers well-equipped with arms and weapons. (Āraṇyaka Parva, 16, 5-18; R.K. Rai, *Mahābhārata Kośa*, p. 100; *Bhāgavata Purāna* I, XI, 12-15; *Harivaṁśa Purāṇa*, 58, 57-66; and *Viṣṇu Purāṇa* V, 23, 14). It was an administrative, religious and commercial centre. The Yādavas had actually settled in Saurāṣṭra with Dvārakā as their headquarters.

In the time of Kṛṣṇa, Dvārakā on the Arabian sea in Gujarat was one of the largest cities of ancient India. According to Purāṇic evidence (*Harivaṁśa*, Viṣṇu Parva, 58, 36; *Bhāgavata* X, 50, 48-54; *Viṣṇu*, V, 23, 13; *Brahma*, 196, 12-15; also Jaina Purāṇas, *Padma*, 109, 27; *Harivaṁśa*, I, 99; and *Mahāpurāṇa*, 58, 83; 71, 27), it was 12 *yojana* (=96 miles) in extent, which has been found absolutely correct on the basis of archaeological excavations and explorations carried out at different parts of the city. In fact, it was divided into four sectors, viz. Mūla-Dvārakā on the south-west coast of Saurāṣṭra (Kaṭhiāwāḍ), about 5 km away from Prabhāsapattan (in the Una Taluka of Jūnāgaṛh district); modern Dvārakā situated on the bank of Gomatī stream where it flows into the Arabian Sea; Beṭ-Dvārakā (an island having a circuit of 12 km), about 30 km north of modern Dvārakā on the western coast of Saurāṣṭra; and Prabhāsatīrtha near Somanāth. Mūla-Dvārakā is traditionally believed to be the most ancient or original Dvārakā of Kṛṣṇa. Modern Dvārakā (also called Gomatī Dvārakā) was not only the seat of government or political capital but also a port and an emporium of trade in his time. Beṭ-Dvārakā was a port city and pleasure resort of Kṛṣṇa. Modern Dvārakā and Beṭ-Dvārakā saw the major settlements of the Yādavas. Gomatī-Dvārakā and Beṭ-Dvārakā were politically and culturally connected with each other at that time. (For full details of Mathurā and Dvārakā, the first and the second political capitals of the Yādavas led by Kṛṣṇa see G.P. Singh, *Republics, Kingdoms, Towns and Cities in Ancient India*, pp. 8-11, 199-201; and *Early Indian Historical Tradition and Archaeology*, pp. 61-73.)

The Yādavas in Dvārakā maintained their old republican tradition of Mathurā under the leadership of Kṛṣṇa. Their life under the new republican set-up was prosperous. But thirty-six years after the Mahābhārata war a fratricidal strife ensued among them in Prabhāsatīrtha in which practically the entire Yādava males were killed as recorded in the *Mahābhārata* (Mausala Parva, 2, 1-20; 3, 1-22; 4, 33, 36 & 41; Ch. 5; 6, 1-15; 7, 9-22) and one of the Purāṇas (*Viṣṇu*, V, 37, 40-50). Kṛṣṇa passed away in Prabhāsatīrtha itself just at the commencement of the Kaliyuga (Kali Age). After his death, the confederacy of the Yādavas naturally got dissolved. And the whole of Dvārakā city except for his palace sank into the sea because of its tidal waves or rise in its general water level as mentioned in the *Mahābhārata* (Mausala Parva, 8, 4-11, 32-47, 58-74; Aśvamedha Parva, 84, 13-16) as well as the Purāṇas (*Viṣṇu,* V, 37, 36, 59; V, 38, 9-10; and *Bhāgavata,* XI, 7, 3; XIII, 12, 60). The materials discovered at Dvārakā fix a date for the inundation of the city — between "1500 and 1300 BCE" — before its submerging into the sea. We learn from the *Mahābhārata* (Mahāprasthānika Parva, I, 43) that the Pāṇḍavas in the course of their wanderings beheld the sunken city in the sea (Arabian) with their own eyes. They also saw some of the pillars of the city floating on the surface of the sea water. The city remained submerged under the sea water until its final archaeological discovery in 1987-88.

On the basis of results obtained from the deep vertical excavation carried out in 1962-63 near the Dvārakādhīśa temple jointly with the Department of Archaeology, Gujarat, H.D. Sankalia has drawn the conclusion that there were six habitations or six Dvārakās, and the foundation of the first city of Dvārakā on the sea or on the site of modern Dvārakā goes just before or around the beginning of the Christian era and not much earlier. The different phases of settlements at Dvārakā continued up to the seventh-eighth century CE. He further adds that "Dvārakā . . . was twice submerged into the sea and, therefore, the earlier Dvārakā belonged to Śrī Kṛṣṇa . . . the earliest Dvārakā was found at least in the second-first century BCE-CE. . . ." ("Antiquity of Modern Dvārakā in Literature and Archaeology," in his *Aspects of Indian History and Archaeology,* pp. 191-201.) He asserts that "Even a small and limited excavation at Dvārakā . . . has shown that the stories in the Purāṇas about the city being once submerged in the sea are true. However, this event took place not some

5,000 years ago, as popularly believed, but only about the beginning of the Christian era." ("Archaeology and Tradition," in Ibid., p. 280). The dates put forward by him about the antiquity of Dvārakā city of Kṛṣṇa's time can fairly be disputed.

S.R. Rao, a well-known marine archaeologist, and his team, taking clues from the *Mahābhārata* that Dvārakā was situated at the point where the river Gomatī meets the western sea, further conducted excavation in 1979 in the forecourt or precinct of famous Dvārakādhīśa temple situated near the delta of the Gomatī. The remains discovered from here on the whole belonged to the period ranging from 1500 BCE to the ninth century CE. The remains of some ancient temples with their walls and sculptures intact, some red polished ware, and the copper coins of the third phase of settlement dated to first century BCE were also found. Altogether there were eight phases of settlements at the site. What is most significant is that a pottery found at the site has been dated by one of the most scientific methods of dating (*Thermo-Luminescence*) to about 1500 BCE and it is claimed that it belonged to Kṛṣṇa's era — "1500 BCE" which is considered by them as the date of the Mahābhārata war. Inspired by the initial success they decided to continue the search for the lost capital city of Kṛṣṇa just off the two main temples in the township. Keeping in view the fact stated in the *Mahābhārata* and Purāṇas that Kṛṣṇa's Dvārakā city covered an area of 12 *yojana* (48 *kosa* = 96 miles) they decided to make search for the city under the sea water which began in 1982.

A significant breakthrough was achieved in the field of discovery of sunken Dvārakā city and other remains when a marine archaeological exploration work was undertaken by a team of marine archaeologists from National Institute of Oceanography, Goa, led by S.R. Rao in 1982 at the sea-coast of Dvārakā and Beṭ-Dvārakā (both being connected with the *Mahābhārata* and Kṛṣṇa). During 1982-88, altogether six attempts were made by them in this direction, and ultimately in the sixth attempt (November 1987 – February 1988) S.R. Rao with the help of two of his associates, M.P. Mishra and S. Bandodkar, succeeded in discovering the remains of Kṛṣṇa's city of Dvārakā by diving deep under the water in the vast Arabian sea just off the coast of Dvārakā. S.R. Rao held that the city was submerged by the Arabian sea a few years (thirty-six years) later than the Bhārata battle ("1500-1400 BCE") or "3,500 years ago." The remains of an inner and outer fortifications of the city, two main gates (inner and outer) attached to the fort-walls flanked by a circular bastion of massive blocks of sandstone and that of pillars (bearing decorative designs) of a stone temple within the inner fortifications and other structures were discovered from deep below the sea water, (see Gunakar Mule, "Kahān thī Śrī Kṛṣṇa kī Dvārakā?," *Gagananchal,* ed. G.K. Mathur, Bharatiya Sanskritika Sambandh Parishad, Delhi, 1987, 10, 3, pp. 8-15; *The Hindu,* Gurgaon, 7 February, 1988; *The Indian Express,* Delhi, 6 March, 1988).

The archaeological finds from Beṭ-Dvārakā, 30 km north of Dvārakā, include the inner and outer fortifications of a city extending landward and seaward up to 4 km along the eastern coast (described in the *Mahābhārata* as *varidurga,* i.e. outer-fortress and *udhadhi-madhyasthāna,* i.e. place in the sea) which were submerged because of the rise in the geneal sea-level at that time, nine courses of stone masonry of the massive fort wall, four three-holed stone anchors, various shells bearing the engravings of lotus (*padma*) which were used as seals for various purposes by the dwellers and the rulers of Dvārakā, the remains of the temples and palaces of Kṛṣṇa's time and many other antiquities and monuments. In Beṭ-Dvārakā, according to Rao, there were three settlements, of the pre-*Mahābhārata* (before *c.* 1500 BCE), the *Mahābhārata* (*c.* 1500–1400 BCE) and the post-*Mahābhārata* (third century BCE onwards) periods. The former two are believed to have been engulfed by the sea. While placing the settlement at Beṭ-Dvārakā of the *Mahābhārata* phase between *c.* 1500–1400 BCE, he has put emphasis on *c.* 1424 BCE as the date of the war. There are several old sites in Somanāth and Saurāṣṭra peninsula whose remains still lie submerged under the sea water.

It is striking to note that some of the shells with lotus (*padma*) engraved on them (used as seals) discovered by Rao from Beṭ-Dvārakā find description in the *Mahābhārata.* A verse from the Āraṇyaka Parva (80, 83) bears an eloquent testimony to the fact that in Dvāravatī (Dvārakā) seals bearing the representation of *padma* were seen as an utter surprise. The literary and archaeological evidence regarding the seals concerned goes in perfect harmony with each other. But there are certain evidences about the seals which we find only in the *Mahābhārata.* One of the seals bearing the depiction of trident finds mention therein (Āraṇyaka Parva, 80, 84).

As stated before, the seals were used for various purposes. Politically, their use was determined according to emerging situations. At one stage, Kṛṣṇa as a ruler of Dvārakā had ordered that all citizens while entering or leaving the city should carry their seals for showing to the guards, in charge of its security, as a mark of identification. Thus the seals were also used as a security measure in Kṛṣṇa's Dvārakā. This can be testified to by what is recorded in the Āraṇyaka Parva (16, 19) of the *Mahābhārata.* We find that Śālva, a king of Mārttikavata or Śaubhanagara (Śālvadeśa or Śālvapura corresponding to Bairat in Jaipur, the erstwhile capital of Matsyas) attacked Dvārakā to retaliate the death of his friend

Śiśupāla (a king of Cedi) at the hands of Kṛṣṇa. He entered into a battle with Andhaka-Vṛṣṇis but was ultimately killed by Kṛṣṇa (Ibid., 15, 1-22; 16, 1-4, 13, 16-23; 17, 1-33; 18, 1-24; also chs. 19-21). This invasion created a fear-psychosis of insecurity among the inhabitants of the city. And thus the city was made equipped with arms and weapons, well guarded by soldiers, to defend it against any possible future invasion. (Ibid., 16, 14-18). In order to make distinction between the friends and foes with the help of seals, Kṛṣṇa made it a rule that while entering or leaving the city those who showed the seals to its guards were to be taken as friends and those who could not while doing so as foes.

The economic value of the seals (*mudrā*) in Kṛṣṇa's Dvārakā has been sufficiently highlighted in the *Harivaṁśa* (Viṣṇu Parva, 58, 57-66). The evidence adduced in the text gives us an impression that the seals made from marine shells (called *śaṅkha*) were used to regulate and control the market economy. They were the stabilizer of finance. That is why they have been called *vītarakṣaka.* They served the purpose of a standard currency because of availability of plenty of shells there. They had their own market value. They were the chief means of transaction for the traders in the market. The poverty and richness of the people were greatly determined by these seals. The purchasing capacity of the people largely depended on the possession of these seals. In order to make the city prosperous and improve the economic condition of its Yādava population, Kṛṣṇa greatly encouraged the free flow of such seals in the market. During his time, quite a good number of poor people in Dvārakā city became rich through these seals. As a matter of fact, the financial stability of the whole population of the city entirely depended on the possession of these seals. The *Padma Purāṇa* (Svargakhaṇḍa, 24, 14-16) also contains a passage about these seals. About 1½ miles away from Kṛṣṇa's palace at Beṭ-Dvārakā, there was a place called Śaṅkhodvāratīrtha where the work of discovering the shells from the sea and making seals from them was carried out by the people on a large scale during the time of Kṛṣṇa. (For details see G.P. Singh "A Fresh Literary Discovery of the Seals of Dvārakā in the Epic Age: A Supplement to Archaeological Discovery," in his *Republics, Kingdoms, Towns and Cities in Ancient India*, pp. 217-21.)

A seal made from a shell bearing the image of a three-headed creature with the heads of bull, unicorn and goat, and some other smaller rectangular seals with perforated button at the back discovered from the Beṭ-Dvārakā do not find any description in the *Mahābhārata* and Purāṇas.

The archaeological rediscovery of lost Dvārakā city of Kṛṣṇa not only proves the existence of the city but also the historicity of Kṛṣṇa and of the details of the subject provided in the *Mahābhārata* and Purāṇas.

There is an archaeological evidence to prove that the sites of ancient cities of Mūla-Dvārakā (founded by Kṛṣṇa himself), Mādhavapura (where Kṛṣṇa married Rukmiṇī), Sudāmāpurī (the residence of Kṛṣṇa's friend Sudāmā), etc. are located in the south-eastern corner of Kāṭhiāwāḍ. (*Archaeological Survey of India, Report*, vol. XLV (Imperial Series), introd. p. I.) Further, the remains of the temple of Raṇachoṛajī (another name of Kṛṣṇa, for he left Mathurā without fighting and defeating his enemy Jarāsandha, the king of Magadha), the palaces of Kṛṣṇa and his favourite queens, Rādhā and Rukmiṇī, many other temples in a village on the northern side of Beṭ-Dvārakā and that of a temple of Śaṅkhanārāyaṇa in Śaṅkhodvāratīrtha, about 1½ miles away from Kṛṣṇa's palace (where Śaṅkhāsura was killed by Kṛṣṇa) are associated with the past life of Kṛṣṇa and his family members and the events of their period.

On the authority of Megasthenes, the Greek historian of the fourth century BCE, Arrian, the Greek historian of the second century CE, in his *Indika* (Pt. I) explicitly states that Herakles (Kṛṣṇa) was held in especial honour by the *Sourasenoi* (Śūrasenas, the Yādavas of Śūrasena) who possessed two large cities, *Methora* (Mathurā, the capital) and *Kleisobora* (Kṛṣṇapura identical with Vṛndāvana) on the river *Jomanes* (Yamunā) also called *Iobares.* (J.W. McCrindle, *Ancient India as Described by Megasthenes and Arrian,* p. 201, see also pp. 139-40 and note.) Pāṇini, Patañjali and some of the Buddhist and Jaina writers also mention Kṛṣṇa and some of the events of his life. The Chinese traveller Yuan Chwang (Hiuen Tsang) of the seventh century CE records in his *Si-yu-ki* (*Travels in India*) that a great war was fought at Kurukṣetra and the bones of the dead warriors lay buried under the soil.

In March 2003, at the CP Art Centre in Chennai, T.K.V. Rajan, a distinguished archaeologist, presented an exhibition titled "In Search of Kṛṣṇa," a well-documented collection of material about the excavations conducted at the various sites connected with the life of Kṛṣṇa and the events of the *Mahābhārata.* Over 35 sites of the *Mahābhārata* have been identifed in the north, all yielding material culture representing Painted Grey Ware (PGW) covering the period *c.* 1000–800 BCE.

In the light of the facts stated above no sensible historian will cast doubt on the historical existence of Kṛṣṇa.

# 4

## Recapitulation and Observation

AFTER having made a thorough investigation into the sources available at our disposal we find that Rāma and Kṛṣṇa were not mythical but historical personages. They occupy very important places in the history of India of the epic age. They left behind an indelible stamp of their personality and glorious deeds on the pages of ancient Indian history dealing with society and culture which the people will remember for ages to come. The presentation of such facts is often mis-construed as an attempt at their glorification. But it is highly unfair to deny the reality of history.

Ayodhyā, the capital of the kingdom of Kosala over which Rāma, the $65^{th}$ king in descent from Ikṣvāku of the Solar dynasty, ruled for a considerable period of time, had already flourished as a city before the former ascended to its throne. During the period concerned the city was known both as Ayodhyā and Sāketa. It was during the Buddhist period that it became more popularly known as Sāketa which, however, does not mean that Ayodhyā as such was not at all in existence during the preceding period. It is also not at all correct to say that Ayodhyā described in the *Rāmāyaṇa* of Vālmīki was not the capital of Kosala kingdom during the time of Rāma. It is also said that Ayodhyā rose into prominence in the age of the Buddha and not in the age of Rāma. Such statements are made by some historians writing of ancient India to deny the primaeval antiquity of Ayodhyā and historicity of Rāma.

Sometimes attempts are made grudgingly and intentionally at the distortion and falsification of history of the age of Rāma. He was, no doubt, one of the ancient rulers of India. Sometimes, under the pretext of the absence of concrete archaeological evidence about him his existence is denied. There are, of course, some archaeological evidences which go in support of the existence of Rāma of Ayodhyā, but we do not possess as much authentic ones as we do in respect of Kṛṣṇa of Dvārakā. However, whatever evidences we have at our disposal are sufficient enough to show that Rāma of Ayodhyā was a historical figure. The existence of kingdoms over which he and his two sons ruled has been archaeologically proved by a noted British historian and archaeologist, A. Cunningham, on the basis of his findings whose details are available in his Archaeological Reports. The places Rāma visited in the course of his wanderings during the exile period have also been traced by some archaeologists. There are some archaeological evidences whose importance cannot be dismissed. These are some of the evidences which definitely go to dissipate the doubts of the historians and politicians concerned about the existence of Rāma.

It can also be established that Kṛṣṇa along with other Yādava tribes especially the Andhakas and Vṛṣṇis first ruled the Śūrasena state with its capital at Mathurā and then at Dvārakā. He gained immense popularity as a chief of the confederacy (*saṁgha*) of the Andhaka-Vṛṣṇis. He headed the republican system of government of the Yādavas of Śūrasena in pre-Bhārata war period. He ruled Dvārakā both in pre- and post-war period until his death. His historicity has already been proved by the archaeological rediscovery of this city.

In the light of the discovery of the facts, all the doubts of historians and politicians concerned about the historicity of

Rāma and Kṛṣṇa may be set at rest. It is altogether a different fact that both of them by virtue of their benevolent deeds and because of their greatness immortalized themselves as gods and found places not only in the temples but also in the hearts of millions and millions of the people of India and outside.

The antiquity of Rāma and Kṛṣṇa cannot be determined with absolute certainty. It may categorically be stated here that the literary evidence cannot be correlated with archaeological data for ascertaining either the age of *Rāmāyaṇa* and *Mahābhārata* or the age of Rāma and Kṛṣṇa. The places described in the *Rāmāyaṇa* and the *Mahābhārata* also cannot be associated or identified with *PGW* period — *c.* 1000-800 BCE (based on Carbon-14 dating). H.D. Sankalia holds that Ayodhyā of the *Rāmāyaṇa* in a true historical persptive was a well-fortified city ascribed to *c.* 1000–800 BCE. In 1967, he discovered there sherds of PGW. (Cf. *Annals of the Bhandarkar Oriental Research Institute,* Poona, LVIII-LIX, 1977-78, pp. 893-919.) Some of the objects discovered by B.B. Lal in the course of archaeological excavations at different places in Ayodhyā between 1975 and 1980 (already noted before) have been dated *c.* 800–700 BCE with the help of two different methods, Carbon-14 test and Thermoluminescence test conducted in Physical Research Laboratory, Ahmedabad. The dates obtained do not represent Ayodhyā of the age of *Rāmāyaṇa.* Hastināpura described in the *Mahābhārata* was the chief capital city of the Kuru kingdom in the pre- and post-war period. The excavations were carried out at the site by B.B. Lal in 1950-52. He has ascribed the first phase of settlement there to OCP period (*c.* 1200 BCE) and the second phase to PGW period (*c.* 1100–800 BCE). (*Ancient India, Bulletin of the Archaeological Survey of India,* New Delhi, Nos. 10 & 11. 1954-55, pp. 5ff.) It is very difficult to say as to how far do the dates suggested by him represent the real age of the site. The *Mahābhārata* period has been connected by some historians of ancient India with Later Vedic Phase ascribed by them to "*c*. 1000–600 BCE." But we do not find any basis for it. The reliability of radiocarbon dating has become a debatable topic amongst the archaeologists themselves, the reason being that the antiquity and identity of samples tested in the laboratories cannot be ascertained with full amount of confidence. It is believed by the archaeologists themselves that the radiocarbon dates are younger than the real age. (For details see *Purātattva, Journal of the Indian Archaeological Society*, No. 9, 1977-78, pp. 64-81; *Antiquity: A Quarterly Review of Archaeology*, Cambridge; vol. LII, p. 117; *American Antiquity*, vol. 43, 1978, pp. 231-44; and *East and West*, Rome, vol. 25, pp. 111-45.) Thus, we cannot depend on C-14 dates of PGW phase of Ayodhyā and Hastināpura for deciding the antiquity of Rāma and Kṛṣṇa respectively.

Likewise, no definite date of the Mahābhārata war in which Kṛṣṇa himself played a vital role can be suggested. The dates of the said war range from *c*. 6000 BCE to *c*. 800 BCE which include the traditional date 3138 BCE, 2800 BCE — *Thermo-Luminescence* dating of blood-stained iron arrows, spearheads, etc. found in the course of excavations at Kurukṣetra, site of the war *c*. 1922 BCE and *c*. 1472–1370 BCE based on Purāṇic data, 1500–1400 BCE and 1400–1000 BCE, dates of some historians and archaeologists, and Carbon-14 dates 900–800 BCE obtained by some archaeologists. I have been consistently pointing out that all the dates before 326 BCE given in ancient Indian history are hypothetical.

One of the root causes of doubting the historicity of Rāma and Kṛṣṇa is the general misconception that the epics — *Rāmāyaṇa* of Vālmīki and *Mahābhārata* — and Purāṇas are more mythical than historical. But the fact remains that they are partly legendary and partly historical. It is worthy of remark that any literary text cannot be purely a historical record because of the literary tradition of historiography prevailing in the contemporary age.

The conflict between history and mythology sometimes, of course, stands as a barrier in our way of reconstruction of history of the past. But we can overcome this problem with the help of those available evidences which bear the stamp of historicity.

The ancient Indian texts need careful study for debunking the truth from the myth. It is not fair to pass judgement about any work without going through its contents.

The *Rāmāyaṇa* has been called a *purātana itihāsa* (ancient history) by its author (Vālmīki) himself (Yuddhakāṇḍa, 131, 116); it has also been called a historical epic (Bālakāṇḍa, p. 13, note 2) which can be justified by the historical and quasi-historical materials it contains. We find in it the historical geography and cultural ethnography of contemporary India, the dynastic history of the Solar and Lunar families, the historical details of various kingdoms and principalities, towns and cities, polity and administration, the condition of the Āryan society, life and culture of some tribal people including the Kirātas, etc. The genealogy of the kings of Ayodhyā (the capital of Kosala kingdom) from Ikṣvāku down to Rāma of the Solar family, a brief history of the Videha dynasty and the Vaiśala dynasty with the genealogy of the former, history of the kings of Lunar family, and the history of various other kingdoms and dynasties are preserved in it. Rāma is depicted in it as a real character. The entire details about him as one of the kings of Kośala with its capital at Ayodhyā are provided in it. It is nothing but a fanciful notion that he was an imaginary character. It is also not correct to say that there is no historical proof of his existence. "The *Rāmāyaṇa* is superb indeed both as regards form and matter, and it portrays ideal characters in almost all aspects of human life. . . . Rāma was a real person, who belonged to the royal Ikṣvāku house of Ayodhyā . . . ," writes R.S. Tripathi in his *History of Ancient India* (pp. 63, 65).

R.C. Dutt (*A History of Civilisation in Ancient India,* p. 211), S.C. De (*Historicity of Rāmāyaṇa and the Indo-Āryan Society in India and Ceylon,* pp. 37ff), Monier-Williams (*Indian Epic Poetry,* p. 8) and Jacobi (*Das Rāmāyaṇa,* pp. 5ff) are of the view that the *Rāmāyaṇa* has a historical basis.

The *Mahābhārata* was originally composed by Vyāsa three years after the war. In the text itself (Ādi Parva, I, 24-25, 48, 52; 56, 18-20, 25-27; Svargārohaṇa Parva, 5, 39, 43), it has been repeatedly called an *itihāsa* (history). It was also called *Bhārata Itihāsa* because of being a history of Bharat dynasty. The text bespeaks that this *itihāsa,* full of the details of valuable subjects, is the best of the *itihāsa*s (Ādi Parva, 1, 61; 2, 31-33; also 56, 15-16). Later many stories and contemporary events were incorporated and many additions were made to it. This practice continued till the Gupta period. The text in the present enlarged form is divided into eighteen *parvan*s or books. The *Mahābhārata* and the Purāṇas are not the productions of one brain or of one period.

According to V.S. Agrawala (*Bhārata Sāvitrī,* based on his in-depth study of the *Mahābhārata,* vol. I, pp. 27-30; vol. 3, pp. 230-39, 262-64), Umashankar Dikshita (*Maharṣi Vedavyāsa: A Historical and Cultural Biography* p. 13) and K.K. Dasgupta ("Historical Biography in Sanskrit Literature," in *Historical Biography in Indian Literature,* ed. S.P. Sen, p. 6), the *Mahābhārata* is an important work from a historical point of view, and it has its own historical value. C.V. Vaidya (*The Mahābhārata : A*

*Criticism*, pp. 37ff, 50ff, 59) considers it both an epic and a history.

The *Mahābhārata* as a whole contains valuable historical information about the Āryans and non-Āryans, dynasties of the Lunar race of pre- and post-war periods, kingdoms and republics, kingship and state, towns and cities, the contemporary social, religious and cultural life of the people, etc. The text also throws light on different aspects of the life of Kṛṣṇa. Estimating its historical value R.S. Tripathi wrote, ". . . there are undoubted deviations from historical accuracy in the *Mahābhārata*, but the central theme is authentic, and its characters . . . are by no means imaginary." (Ibid., pp. 68-69.)

The Purāṇas originally called *Itihāsa Saṁhitā* also deal with historical subjects. Kings and rulers and kingdoms and dynasties of pre- and post-Bhārata war periods, kingship and state, polity and administration, towns and cities, etc. are described therein in detail. They abound in valuable information particularly about the political history of ancient India to the twelfth century CE. Of the eighteen Purāṇas, the six — *Vāyu, Matsya, Viṣṇu, Brahmāṇḍa, Bhāgavata* and *Bhaviṣya* — are very important from a historical point of view. The dynastic genealogies and chronology of the kings of Bimbisāra, Śiśunāga, Nanda, Maurya, Śuṅga and Kāṇva dynasties of Magadha and those of the Sātavāhana kings of the Deccan given in the aforesaid six Purāṇas are of exceptional value. The *Bhaviṣya Purāṇa* in particular contains information about some aspects of the history of pre- and post-Harṣa period. (For historical contents of the epics and the Purāṇas see G.P. Singh, *Ancient Indian Historiography : Sources and Interpretations*, pp. 21-51.)

The information provided in the Purāṇas about Rāma and Kṛṣṇa are historically and archaeologically well tested. For

Rāma we can place our reliance on the testimony of the *Rāmāyaṇa* and Purāṇas and for Kṛṣṇa the *Mahābhārata* and Purāṇas.

Literature and archaeology are two important sources of our knowledge of ancient Indian history and culture. In some cases both are supplementary and confirmatory to each other. But there are so many historical facts in ancient Indian literature (Sanskrit, Buddhist and Jaina) which have not yet been archaeologically confirmed, but it does not necessarily mean that they are unhistorical or mythical. Historical information can be culled from both literary and archaeological sources. Both are of equal importance.

It is true that we do not have as much substantial archaeological evidence about Rāma as we do have about Kṛṣṇa. But it does not imply that all that recorded in the *Rāmāyaṇa* and Purāṇas about the former as a king of Ayodhyā are unworthy of credence.

Notwithstanding the new discoveries and findings about Rāma and Kṛṣṇa, some historians writing of ancient India, some politicians and some scholars and savants still question their historicity and doubt the historical value of the epics and Purāṇas because of their obsession with the views they hold within the conceptualized framework and their pre-conceived notion or make believe.

It is the historical truth that prevails, and not any postulation or supposition.

The historicity of Rāma described in the *Vālmīki-Rāmāyaṇa* and Purāṇas as well as the historicity of Kṛṣṇa described in the *Mahābhārata* and Purāṇas can be proved beyond doubt with the help of available literary, historical, archaeological and scientific evidence.

# Select Bibliography

## Literary Sources

### THE VEDA

*Ṛgveda Saṁhitā*, ed. with Sāyaṇa's comm. by F. Max Müller, 2nd edn., London, 1890-92; trans. by R.T.H. Griffith, Benares, 1896-97; trans. by H.H. Wilson, 6 vols., London, 1866-88; ed. with Hindi trans. and Sāyaṇa's comm. by R. Sharma Ācārya, 4 vols., Baveilly, 1974-75.

### THE EPICS

*Mahābhārata*, ed. with Hindi trans. by S. Damodar Satavalekar and Shri Shrutishil Sharma, Paradi (Gujarat): Ādi Parva, 1968; Anuśāsana Parva, 1978; Āraṇyaka Parva, 2 vols., 1969; Āśramavāsika Parva, 1977; Aśvamedhika Parva, 1977; Bhīṣma Parva, 1972; Droṇa Parva, 1975; Karṇa Parva, 1973; Mahāprasthānika Parva, 1977; Mausala Parva, 1977; Sabhā Parva, 1982; Śānti Parva, 2 vols., 1979-80; Svargārohaṇa Parva, 1977; Udyoga Parva, 1969; Virāṭa Parva, 1969;

*Vālmīki-Rāmāyaṇa*, ed. by D.R. Mankad, Oriental Research Institute, Baroda, 1965; trans. by R.T.H. Griffith, London, 1870.

———, Ayodhyākāṇḍa, ed. with Hindi trans. by Pt. Akhilananda, Amritsar, vs 2019.

———, Bālakāṇḍa, ed. with Hindi trans. of Yudhiṣṭhira Mīmāṁsaka by Pt. Akhilananda, Amritsar, vs 2025.

———, Kiṣkindhākāṇḍa, ed. with Hindi trans. by Pt. Akhilananda, Amritsar, vs 2021.

———, Uttarakāṇḍa, cf. *Vālmīki-Rāmāyaṇa*, ed. by D.R. Mankad.

———, Yuddha (Laṅkā) Kāṇḍa, text with Hindi trans. of Pt. Vijayapala, Bahalagarh, vs 2029.

PURĀṆAS

*Agni Purāṇa*, ed. by H.N. Apte, Ānandāśrama Sanskrit series, Poona, 1900; ed. by R.L. Mitra, Bibliotheca Indica Series (BIS), Asiatic Society of Bengal (ASB), Calcutta, 1893-79; text with Hindi trans. of T. Jha and G.S. Tripathi, Prayag, 1986; Eng. trans. by M.N. Dutt, 2 vols. Calcutta, 1903-04.

*Bhāgavata Purāṇa*, text with Hindi trans. and annotation, 2 vols. 8th edn., Gorakhpur, Saṁvat, 2040; ed. with Eng. trans. by C.L. Goswami, 2 Pts., 2nd edn., Gorakhpur, 1982.

*Bhaviṣya Purāṇa*, Venkatesvara Press, Bombay, 1910; ed. with Hindi trans. by R. Sharma Ācārya, 2 vols., Baveilly, 1978.

*Brahma Purāṇa*, ed. by H.N. Apte, Ānandāśrama Sanskrit Series, Poona, 1895; text with Hindi trans. of T. Jha. Prayag, 1976.

*Brahmāṇḍa Purāṇa*, Venkateśvara Press, Bombay, 1913.

*Brahmavaivartta Purāṇa*, ed. with Hindi trans. by T. Jha, Allahabad, 1985.

*Harivaṁśa Purāṇa*, ed. by N. Mukhopadhyaya, ASB, Calcutta, 1858; ed. by R. Kinjawadekar, Poona, 1936; text with Hindi trans. and comm. 4th edn., Gorakhpur, Saṁvat, 2044.

*Kūrma Purāṇa*, ed. with Hindi trans. of Shree Chaudhari Shree Narayana Singh by Anandasvarupa Gupta, Varanasi, 1972.

*Matsya Purāṇa*, Ānandāśrama Sanskrit Series, Poona, 1907; text with Hindi trans. 2 vols. Gorakhpur, 1985; ed. with trans. of various Oriental scholars and notes of B.C. Majumdar, S.C. Vasu, H.H. Wilson, Bentley, Wilford and others by J.D. Akhtar, vol. I, *Sacred Books of the Aryan Series*, Delhi, 1972.

*Padma Purāṇa*, ed. by V.N. Mandalika, 4 vols., Ānandāśrama Sanskrit Series, Poona, 1893-94; "Svargakhaṇḍa," ed. by Asoka Chatterjee Sastri, Varanasi, 1972.

*Skanda Purāṇa*, ed. by Vasudeva Sastri, 3 Pts., Ānandāśrama Sanskrit Series, Poona, 1893.

*Vāyu Purāṇa*, ed. by R.L. Mitra, 2 vols., BIS, ASB, Calcutta, 1880-88; Ānandāśrama Sanskrit Series, Poona, 1905; text with Hindi trans. of R.P. Tripathi Sastri, Prayag, 1987.

*Viṣṇu Purāṇa*, ed. by J. Vidyasagara, Calcutta, 1882; trans. by M.N. Dutt, Calcutta, 1894; trans. by H.H. Wilson, Calcutta, 1961; text with Hindi trans. of Muni Lal Gupta, 9th edn., Gorakhpur, Samvat, 2041.

*Viṣṇudharmottara Mahāpurāṇa*, Venkatesvara Press, Bombay, 1912; ed. by P. Shah, Baroda, 1961.

OTHER SANSKRIT WORKS

*Arthaśāstra of Kauṭilya*, ed. by R. Shamasastry, Mysore, 1909; trans. by R. Shamasastry, Bangalore, 1915; ed. with Hindi trans. by Vachaspati Gairola, Varanasi, 1984.

*Aṣṭādhyāyī of Pāṇini* (*Sūtrapāṭha* with *Gaṇas* and *Vārttikas*), ed. by S.C. Śāstrī, Trichinopoly, 1912; ed. by B.M. Sharma, Varanasi, 1948; ed. with Eng. trans. by S.C. Vasu, 7 vols. Allahabad, 1891-98, rept., 1929.

*Mahābhāṣya of Patañjali*, ed. by F. Kielhorn, 3 vols., Bombay Sanskrit Series, Bombay, 1880-85.

*Raghuvaṁśa of Kālidāsa, with Mallinātha's comm. Sañjīvanī*, ed. by K.M. Joglekar, Bombay, 1916; ed. with Eng. trans. and notes by M.R. Kale, rept. edn., Delhi, 1972.

BUDDHIST WORKS

## *Canonical*

*Dīgha-Nikāya*, ed. by T.W. Rhys Davids and J.E. Carpenter, 3 vols., Pali Text Society (PTS), London, 1890-1911, rept., 1947-60; trans. by T.W. and C.A.F. Rhys Davids (*The Dialogues of the Buddha*), 3 vols., PTS, London, 1899-1921; trans. by Rahula Sāṅkṛtyāyana and Jagadish Kashyapa, Banaras, 1936.

## *Non-Canonical*

*Avadānaśataka*, ed. by J.S. Speyer, 2 vols., St. Petersburg, 1906.

*Buddhacarita* of Aśvaghoṣa, ed. and trans. by E.H. Johnston, 2 vols., 2nd edn., Delhi, 1972; trans. (cantos I-XVII) by E.B. Cowell, in *Sacred Books of the East*, XLIX, I, Oxford, 1894, rept. Delhi, 1972.

*Dīpavaṁśa*, ed. and trans. by H. Oldenberg, London, 1879, rept. Delhi, 1982.

*Mahāvaṁśa*, ed. by W. Geiger, PTS, London, 1908, rept. 1958; trans. by W. Geiger and M.H. Bode, PTS, London, 1912, rept. 1950, trans. of both *Dīpavaṁśa* and *Mahāvaṁśa* by E.M. Coomaraswamy (*The Dīpavaṁśa and Mahāvaṁśa and their Historical Development in Ceylon*). Colombo, 1908.

## JAIN WORKS

### *Non-Canonical*

*Abhidhānacintāmaṇi* of Hemacandra, Ahmedabad, vs 2013.

*Ādi Purāṇa* of Jinasena III, ed. by Pannalal Jain, 1st edn. Bhāratiya Jñānapīṭha (BGP), Kāśī, 1951.

*Harivaṁśa Purāṇa* of Jinasena II, ed. by Pannalal Jain, BGP, Kāśī, 1962.

*Mahāpurāṇa* of Puṣpadanta, ed. by D.K. Jain 4 vols., Manikchand Digambara Jain Granthmala Series (MDJG), Bombay, 1979-83; ed. by P.L. Vaidya, 3 vols., Bombay, 1937-41.

*Padma Purāṇa* of Ravisena, ed. by Pannalal Jain, 3 vols., 1st edn., BGP, Kāśī, 1958-59.

*Uttarapurāṇa* of Guṇabhadra, ed. by Pannalal Jain, 1st edn., BGP, Kāśī, 1952, revd. edn. Kāśī, 1954.

*Vividhatīrthakalpa* of Jinaprabhasūri, Bombay, 1934.

## GREEK SOURCES

Arriaṇ, *Anabasis of Alexander* (*History of Alexander's Expedition*), ed. by A.G. Roos, Leipzig, 1907.

———, *Indika* (the treatise on India), Pt. I, Chaps. I-XVII, Leipzig, 1867.

———, Eng. trans. of both *Anabasis* and *Indika*, by E.J. Chinnock, London, 1893.

Megasthenes, *Indika*, its Fragments collected and ed. by E.A. Schwanbeck, *Megasthenis Indica*, Bonn, 1846.

McCrindle, J.W. *Ancient India as Described by Megasthenes and Arrian* (trans. of the Fragments of the *Indika* of Megasthenes and of the first part of the *Indika* (Chs. I-XVII) of Arrian) 1st edn., London, 1877.

## CHINESE WORKS

Fa-hien, *Fo-Kwo-Ki*, Eng. trans. by H.A. Giles, *A Record of the Buddhistic Kingdoms* (*an Account of the Travels of Fa-hien*), 1st edn., Cambridge, 1923, rept. Varanasi, 1972; Eng. trans. by J. Legge, *A Record of the Buddhistic Kingdoms (an Account of the Travels of Fa-hien,)* 1st edn., Oxford, 1886, rept. Delhi, 1972.

Hiuen Tsang, *Si-Yu-Ki,* Eng. trans. by T. Watters, *On Yuan Chwang's Travels in India,* ed. by T.W. Rhys Davids and S.W. Bushell, 2 vols., RAS, London, 1904-05, 2nd Indian edn., Delhi, 1973.

## Coins and Inscriptions

Allan, J., *A Catalogue of the Indian Coins in the British Museum, Ancient India,* London, 1936.

Cunningham, A., *Coins of Ancient India from the Earliest Times down to the Seventh Century* CE, London, 1891, rept. Varanasi, 1971.

Sircar, D.C. (ed.), *Select Inscriptions Bearing on Indian History and Civilization,* vol. I (from the sixth century BCE to the sixth century CE), Calcutta, 1965.

Smith, V.A., *Catalogue of the Coins in the Indian Museum,* Calcutta, vol. I, *Coins of Ancient India,* Oxford, 1906, rept. Varanasi, 1972.

**Modern Works**

Agrawala, V.S., *Bhārata Sāvitrī* (based on his in-depth historical study of the *Mahābhārata*), vols. 1 and 2, and 2nd edn., Delhi, 1977, vol. 3, 1st edn., Delhi, 1968

——— *India as known to Pāṇini* (*A Study of the Cultural Material in the Aṣṭādhyāyī*), Varanasi, 1963.

Banerji, S.C., *Kālidāsa-Kośa,* Varanasi, 1968.

Cunningham, A., *The Ancient Geography of India,* 1st end., London, 1871, rept. Varanasi, 1979.

Dasgupta, K.K., "Historical Biography in Sanskrit Literature," *in Historical Biography in Indian Literature,* ed., S.P. Sen, Calcutta, 1979, pp. 3-28.

De, S.C., *Historicity of Rāmāyaṇa and the Indo-Āryan Society in India and Ceylon,* Delhi, 1976.

Dikshita, U.S., *Maharṣi Vedavyāsa: A Historical and Cultural Biography,* Varanasi, 1968.

Dutt, R.C., *A History of Civilization in Ancient India based on Sanskrit Literature,* vol. I (*c.* 2000-320 BCE), Mymensingh, 1888, Calcutta, 1899, rept. Delhi, 1972.

Ghoshal, U.N., *A History of Indian Political Ideas,* Bombay, 1959.

Jacobi, H., *Das Rāmāyaṇa,* Bonn, 1893.

Jain, J.C., *Life in Ancient India as Depicted in the Jaina Canon and Commentaries (6th Century BCE to 17th Century CE)*, Delhi, 1984.

Jayaswal, K.P., *Hindu Polity: A Constitutional History of India in Hindu Times*, pts. I & II, Bangalore, 1981.

Keith, A.B., *History of Sanskrit Literature*, Oxford, 1920, rept. Delhi, 1973.

Law, B.C., "Countries and Peoples of India" (Epic and Paurāṇic Sources), *Annals of the Bhandarkar Oriental Research Institute*, vol. XVII, Pt. III, 1935-36, pp. 225ff.

———, "Śrāvastī in Ancient Indian Literature," *Memoirs of the Archaeological Survey of India*, no. 50 (Delhi, 1935), pp. 9ff.

———, "The Kosalas in Ancient India," *Indian Historical Quarterly*, vol. I, nos. 1-2 (new rept. Delhi, 1979), pp. 139-65.

———, An article on Ayodhyā in *Journal of Ganganath Jha Research Institute*, vol. I, pp. 423-43.

———, *Geographical Essays Relating to Ancient Geography of India*, Delhi, 1976.

———, *Geography of Early Buddhism*, Varanasi, 1973.

Macdonell, A.A., *History of Sanskrit Literature*, 1st edn., Oxford, 1899, 3rd Indian edn., Delhi, 1972.

Malalasekera, G.P., *Dictionary of Pāli Proper Names*, 2 vols. London, 1937-38, rept., Delhi, 1983.

Max Müller, F., *A History of Ancient Sanskrit Literature*, 1st edn., London, 1859, revd. and ed. by S.N. Sastri, Varanasi, 1968.

Mitra, R.L., *Sanskrit Buddhist Literature of Nepal*, Calcutta, 1882.

Pargiter, F.E., *Ancient Indian Historical Tradition*, 1st edn., London, 1922, rept. Delhi, 1972.

———, *The Purāṇa Text of the Dynasties of the Kali Age*, Oxford, 1913, rept. Varanasi, 1962.

Pradhan, S.N., *Chronology of Ancient India*, Varanasi, 1979.

Puri, B.N., *India in the time of Patañjali*, Bombay, 1968.

Rai, R.K., *Vālmīki-Rāmāyaṇa Kośa*, Varanasi, 1965.

———, *Mahābhārata Kośa*, Varanasi, 1982.

Rajaram, N.S., "Distortions of Indian History from Harappa to Ayodhya," *The Astrological Magazine*, Bangalore, vol. 87, no. I, January 1998, p. 76.

Sankalia, H.D., *Aspects of Indian History and Archaeology*, ed. S.P. Gupta and K.S. Ramachandran, Delhi, 1977.

Sen, S.P. (ed.), *Historical Biography in Indian Literature*, Calcutta, 1979.

Sharma, R.P., *Paurāṇic Kośa*, Varanasi, vs 2028.

Singh, G.P., *Early Indian Historical Tradition and Archaeology*, Delhi, 1994.

———, *Ancient Indian Historiography : Sources and Interpretations*, Delhi, 2003.

———, *Republics, Kingdoms, Towns and Cities in Ancient India*, Delhi, 2003.

Smith, V.A., *The Early History of India*, revd. by S.M. Edwards, 4th edn. London, 1967.

Thapar, R., *Ancient Indian Social History*, Hyderabad, 1984.

Tripathi, R.S., *History of Ancient India*, Delhi, 1985.

Vaidya, C.V., *The Mahābhārata : A Criticism*, Delhi, 1966.

Williams, M., *Indian Epic Poetry*, London, 1963.

## Journals and Periodicals

*Ancient India — Bulletin of the Archaeological Survey of India*, New Delhi.

*Annals of the Bhandarkar Oriental Research Institute*, Poona.

*Antiquity — A Quarterly Review of Archaeology*, Cambridge.

*Gagananchal*, Bharatiya Samskritika Sambandha Parisada, Delhi.

*Indian Historical Quarterly*, Calcutta, new reprint, Delhi.

*Journal of the Ganganath Jha Research Institute*, Allahabad.

*Memoirs of the Archaeological Survey of India*, Delhi.

*Purātattva* — Journal of the Indian Archaeological Society.

## Newspapers and Reports

*Archaeological Survey of India, Annual Reports*.

Cunningham's *Reports of Archaeological Survey of India*.

*The Hindu*, Gurgaon, February 07, 1988.

*The Indian Express*, Delhi, March 06, 1988.

